英語長文問題

CROSSOVER

3

Daiichi Gakushusha

本書の使い方
HOW TO USE CROSSOVER

本文の語数と, 本文を読むための目標時間です。
すべての問題を解くための制限時間です。

本文に関連する教科やSDGsを示します。英文を読む力に加え, 他の教科等や社会の諸問題に関する知見を深める問題集です。

レッスンは難易度順に配列しました。
CROSSOVER ③では
350〜500語の英文を中心に収録しています。

英文の選定基準
・他の教科等で学習する内容を含むもの
・SDGsの17の目標に深く関連したもの
・現代的な話題

CROSSOVER ③では
CEFR-A2〜B1レベルを到達目標に設定し,
本文はCEFR-A2〜B1レベルの文法で構成しました。

Lesson 8

語数(速読目標時間)	関連教科	関連 SDGs	得 点
384(3分50秒)	—		
制限時間			
20分			/ 50

1 (1)Many of us know first-hand how the spread of infectious diseases can change societal values and lifestyles. It is not a matter of course to remain healthy, and in fact, it is now a well-known fact that great efforts are needed to protect our health. (2)While it is often assumed that maintaining good health requires individual effort and commitment, and this is certainly true, the role of government is just as important.

2 There was once a disease called the plague that drove the whole world into a fear of death. It was an infectious disease spread by rats that bred in unsanitary city conditions. When the city governments realized how serious it was, they built *sewerage systems and kept the cities hygienic in order to control the breeding of rats and prevent plague outbreaks. From this example, you can see that protecting people's health has a lot to do with town development.

3 (3)The role that town development can play in maintaining people's health is not limited to the fight against infectious diseases. Rather, developed countries that have been able to create clean and hygienic towns are increasingly placing more emphasis on combating lifestyle-related diseases. This includes not only direct measures such as providing people with opportunities for regular health check-ups, but also town development that encourages people to unconsciously choose behaviors that help them stay away from the diseases. For example, data show that people who live near (4)parks exercise 1.2 times more frequently than those who do not. Areas which provide more people with access to parks are likely to contribute to the exercise habits of their residents. Furthermore, the positive role of parks in mental health should also not be forgotten, as they promote interaction between people.

4 Likewise, pollution control is a fundamental role of city government. Among all kinds of pollutants, noise from traffic is one of the most often *overlooked. (5)Airplane noise in particular is the most significant, and some studies have shown that the

英文を読みやすくするため, 脚注では語の注釈を多めに取り上げています。
覚えるべき語句として, 別冊『多読と整理』で同じ語句を取り上げている場合もあります。

二次元コードより, 英文の音声を聞くことができます。

around airports and soundproofing the houses in the *vicinity would be effective.

sewerage system：下水道システム　overlook：…を見落とす　vicinity：近辺, 周辺

20

本文音声

別冊『多読と整理』の使い方
HOW TO USE THE ANNEX

■多読

別冊は見開き構成で, 左ページは
「本文と同じテーマの別英文とその設問」で構成しています。
レポート・広告・記事など, さまざまなテキストタイプの英文を読むことができます。
本文を読む前の背景知識の習得や,
本文を読んだ後の追加演習として使うことができます。

設問に解答するために必要な力を「タグ」として示しました。

▷**知識・技能**：語彙・文法・句読法などに関わる問題です。

▷**主題**：文章全体や段落の主題を把握する問題です。速読スキルを身に付けることができます。

▷**文章展開**：段落どうしのつながりに関わる問題です。

▷**段落構成**：一つの段落の構成などに関わる問題です。パラグラフ・ライティングの参考にすることもできます。

▷**論理**：ディスコースマーカーなどの文脈や，どうしてそう言えるのかを問う問題です。

※その他，問題に応じたタグを付けています。

Which of the following is an example of (1)many of us knowing first-hand how the spread of infectious diseases can change societal values and lifestyles?　▷応用 （8点）

a. AI technology enables cars to drive themselves automatically.

b. Emperor Shomu, wishing to eradicate smallpox, built the great Buddha statue in Nara.

c. Many schools allowed students to attend classes at home during the COVID-19 pandemic.

d. When tuberculosis spread during the Industrial Revolution, many workers set up unions and protested against their poor working conditions.

Translate the following into Japanese: (2)While it is often assumed that maintaining good health requires individual effort and commitment, and this is certainly true, the role of government is just as important.　▷知識・技能 （11点）

In paragraph 3, (3)the role that town development can play in maintaining people's health is not limited to the fight against infectious diseases means _____.　▷段落構成 （8点）

a. towns as well as other groups fight against infectious diseases

b. towns not only fight against infectious diseases, but also against other kind of diseases

c. towns not only fight against infectious diseases, but also help patients recover

d. towns play a role in maintaining people's health and other aspects of their lives

How do (4)parks contribute to people's health? Explain two merits in Japanese.　▷段落構成 （各7点）

設問文は英語で記されています。

よく使われる表現を確認しておきましょう。

According to the text, ...「本文によると，…。」
→本文にない内容を答えないようにしましょう。

Be sure to make ... clear.「…を明確にしなさい。」
→…には指示表現などが入ります。指示表現の内容を明確にして答えましょう。

Explain in detail ....「詳しく説明しなさい。」
→支持文の内容なども交えて，できるだけ詳細に答えましょう。

Translate the following into Japanese: ....「…以下を日本語に翻訳しなさい。」
→なるべく自然な日本語になるよう心がけましょう。

You may choose more than one option.「選択肢を二つ以上選んでもよい。」
→複数解答が正答になる可能性があります。

設問の工夫

・選択式と記述式のバランスに留意しました。
　※記述式は日本語記述が中心です。

・筆者の意図や，「なぜこの語を使ったか」を問う問題を採用しました。
　※モデルとなる本文を多く読むことで，「書く」技能を向上させることもできます。

・本文と日常生活をリンクさせて解答する問題を採用しました。

・選択式では，消去法が最適の解法となる問題を可能なかぎり避けました。

・文法的な正しさや，用語や用法の区別が中心となる問題を避けました。

・和訳問題や，該当箇所を和訳することで答える問題を少なくしました。
　※ ▷知識・技能 タグの問題は和訳問題が中心です。

「解答・解説集」で，選択式の「誤りの選択肢」の根拠や，記述式の「答案例と採点基準」などを示しています。

■整理

右ページは「本文の設問の解答欄」「語句の意味調べ」「要約完成」で構成しています。

本文の設問の解答欄

語句の意味調べ：意味を知っておくべき単語をピックアップしました。取り上げられた単語や表現の意味を書いて覚えましょう（本文の脚注で同じ語句を扱っている場合があります）。

要約完成：本文の概要を理解できたか，要約完成で確認しましょう。ここでは空所補充形式としていますが，慣れてきたら自分で本文を要約し，ストーリーリテリングにも挑戦してみましょう。

CONTENTS

1 Do you get excited when you hear the word "capsule toy"? There are many capsules in a box like a vending machine, and when you insert a coin, one capsule comes out. Each capsule contains a random toy, and it is exciting because you don't know which toy you will get until you actually open it. This is called "gacha-gacha" or
5 simply "gacha" in Japanese.

2 The gacha-gacha system has also become common in online smartphone games recently. People play gacha-gacha to get weapons that make it easier to win the game, or to get characters or avatars that can change their own appearance in the game. Sometimes you can get the item you want in a few attempts, but sometimes you can't
10 get it even after hundreds of attempts.

3 There is a big difference between (1)these two "gacha-gachas." Let me explain with an example. Imagine that you choose one of the capsule toy machines in a shopping street and play with it. There are 100 capsules in the machine, but only one of them contains the toy you want. The probability of getting the toy you want on the first try
15 is 1%. However, it usually doesn't work that way, and you might have to play up to 100 times to get the toy. Conversely, (2)if you try 100 times, you are guaranteed to get the toy you want.

4 But what about the gacha-gacha on online smartphone games? (3)Suppose there is a gacha-gacha in which there is a 1% probability of getting the item you want. Will you
20 always get what you want if you try 100 times? At first glance, you might think so, but actually the answer is no. When you play with the actual capsule toys, the probability of winning increases with each (4)turn. This is because once an item is drawn, it will never be drawn again. However, in the online gacha-gacha, you always have to play with a probability of 1%, and the probability of getting the item you want after
25 attempting 100 times is only about 63%.

5 This probability is perhaps much lower than you expected. To fully enjoy online smartphone games, it may be essential to play gacha-gacha. However, you should also keep in mind that there is a risk of not getting the item you want at all, even if you are not that unlucky.

本文音声

1. Which of the following is closest to the message the author wants to tell us?　🔖主題 (7点)
   a. Online gacha-gacha is more enjoyable than actual capsule toys.
   b. Online gacha-gacha should be prohibited because it causes many troubles for children.
   c. You should realize that there is a risk of not getting the item you want in the online gacha-gacha.
   d. Your luck is the most important factor to fully enjoy online smartphone games.

2. Explain each of (1)these two "gacha-gachas" in brief Japanese.　🔖指示語 (各5点)
   - _____
   - _____

3. Why can the author say (2)if you try 100 times, you are guaranteed to get the toy you want? Explain in Japanese.　🔖論理 (8点)
   _____
   _____

4. Translate the following into Japanese: (3)Suppose there is a gacha-gacha in which there is a 1% probability of getting the item you want.　🔖知識・技能 (8点)
   _____
   _____

5. Which word in the text is closest in meaning to (4)turn? Write one word.　🔖修辞 (7点)
   _____

6. What is the difference between "the 1%" in capsule toy machines and that in online gacha-gacha? Explain in Japanese.　🔖全体把握 (10点)
   _____
   _____
   _____
   _____

1 (1)A drought is primarily a shortage of precipitation, or natural rain or snowfall, that usually occurs over long periods of months or years but can also occur in periods of just days or weeks. In fact, a drought can be declared an emergency in as little as two weeks. In Africa, it is estimated that 90% of all deaths from natural disasters are
5 caused by hunger and thirst due to droughts. Although droughts have occurred throughout history in most parts of the world, recently many of them have been becoming more and more *unpredictable due to climate change. This makes it impossible to plan for water shortages and protect natural water systems such as our rivers, streams, lakes and wetlands.

10 **2** Droughts can harm local lands, agricultural areas and ecosystems and therefore can have a negative impact on local economies. (2)The effects of droughts have been categorized into three basic types: environmental, economic, and social. Environmental impacts include the drying up of wetland areas, increases in the number of forest fires, and the weakening of ecosystems. Economic impacts include
15 lower agricultural production, reduced food output, and less fishing. Social impacts include higher health costs due to excessive heat, higher food costs and shortages of clean water.

3 There are mainly (3)three types of droughts: meteorological, hydrological, and agricultural. Meteorological droughts occur when the natural rain or snowfall are less
20 than normal. Hydrological droughts take place when natural areas of water such as lakes and rivers fall below a certain level. Agricultural droughts are a lack of moisture in the soil, which affects crop and agricultural production.

4 Precipitation occurs when water *vapor from clouds forms rain, snow, *sleet, or *hail. Much of this precipitation falls and *seeps into the surface of the ground, while
25 the remaining precipitation runs off into lakes, rivers and streams. This is "useable water." However, human activities such as deforestation and having too much livestock contribute to losing the usable water. These activities cause the soil to *deteriorate and eventually prevent water from seeping adequately into the ground and being held as ground water. What is worse, less forest produces less water vapor
30 from the trees, resulting in less precipitation, which in turn leads to more droughts.

---

unpredictable：予測不可能の　　vapor：蒸気　　sleet：みぞれ　　hail：ひょう　　seep：しみこむ
deteriorate：劣化する

 本文音声

1. Translate the following into Japanese: (1)A drought is primarily a shortage of precipitation, or natural rain or snowfall, that usually occurs over long periods of months or years but can also occur in periods of just days or weeks. 　　　　　　　　　　　　　　　　　　⟜ 知識・技能 （8点）

_____

_____

2. Which title below best matches each category of (2)the effects of droughts? Match each title with its correct category. 　　　　　　　　　　　　　　　　⟜ 応用 （完答7点）

Environmental (　　)　　　　Economic (　　)　　　　Social (　　)

　　a. Droughts Reducing Rice Production in 2021 by 40%
　　b. Heat Stroke Patients Rapidly Increasing in June 2023
　　c. 24, 300, 000 Hectares of Australian Forest Burnt Down by 2020

3. Which graph below best represents each of the (3)three types of droughts? Choose one for each category. 　　　　　　　　　　　　　　　　⟜ 応用 （完答7点）

Meteorological (　　)　　　　Hydrological (　　)　　　　Agricultural (　　)

a. Price of Tomatoes　　　　b. Water Storage Rate in a Dam 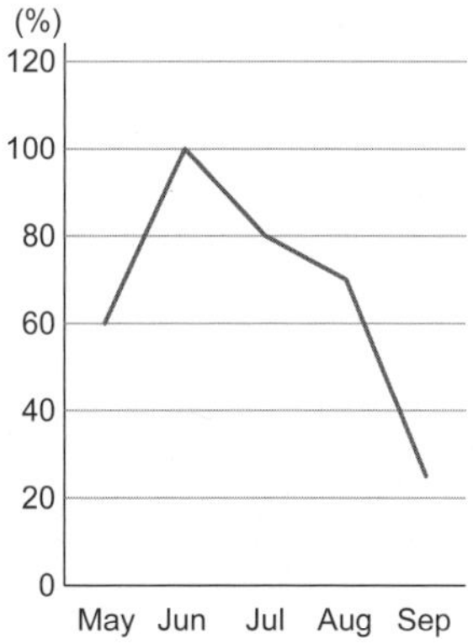　　c. Yearly Precipitation in Sapporo City
　　　(per 1kg)　　　　　　　　　　　　　　　　　　　　　　　　　　　（2020- 2021）

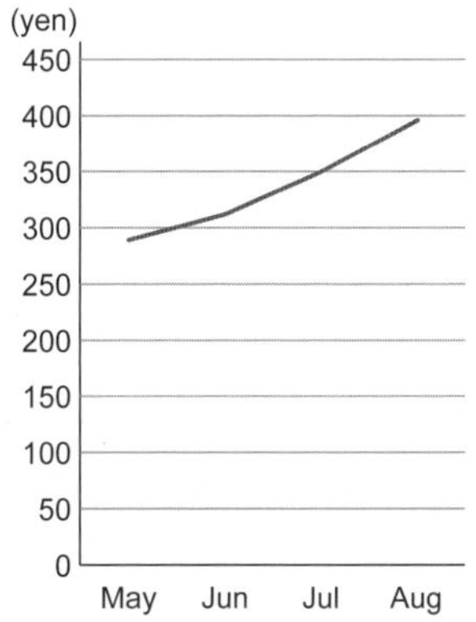

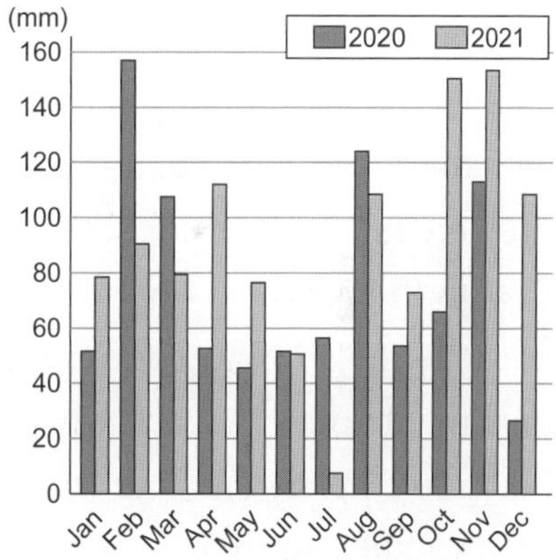

4. There are (3)three types of droughts. What kind of water is lacking in each? Choose the words or phrases from paragraph 4. 　　　　　　　　　　　　⟜ 文章展開 （各6点）

Meteorological 　　_____　　　Hydrological 　　_____
Agricultural 　　_____

5. How does the author think human activities contribute to droughts? Explain in Japanese. 　　　　　　　　　　　　　　　　　　　　　　　⟜ 段落構成 （10点）

_____

_____

1 (1)Many illegal immigrants to the U.S. come from Central and South American countries, crossing the border from Mexico. Most want a better life for their families because of poverty and even violence from *drug cartels and gangs in their home countries. Many workers also travel alone to earn money to send back to their families.
5 There are even children who come by themselves.

2 Children who have been brought to the U.S. illegally by their parents and have grown up there are called "Dreamers." This comes from "(2)the Dream Act," a law that would have created a way for these young immigrants to get U.S. citizenship. Supporters of the Dream Act argue that the Dreamers should be granted American
10 citizenship because: 1) they were not brought to America by their own choice, 2) they have grown up and gone to school in the U.S., 3) they think of themselves as Americans, and 4) they have become productive members of American society. However, opponents to encouraging illegal immigration blocked the Dream Act from becoming a law.

15 **3** In response, in 2012, the Obama administration created (3)the Deferred Action for Childhood Arrivals (DACA) program. DACA gives Dreamers temporary protection against *deportation. They can get permission to work in the U.S. for two years. Dreamers can also apply for permission to leave the U.S. and re-enter, even though they are not legal residents.

20 **4** On the contrary, opponents to the Dream Act say that (4)Dreamers should be forced back to their home countries because giving them a pathway to citizenship would encourage more illegal immigration. They also argue that President Obama exceeded his *authority by creating DACA.

5 Donald Trump, who became president after Barack Obama, began building a wall
25 along the U.S.-Mexico border to make it more difficult to cross illegally. This was not only to stop illegal immigrants but also *drug traffickers who have been involved in violent incidents that have hurt or killed Americans. Joe Biden, who became president after Trump, *halted construction of the wall on his first day as president. This was because he supported a gentler approach to illegal immigration. Many U.S. politicians
30 have long sought a solution to illegal immigration, but they have not yet been able to agree on one.

---

drug cartel：麻薬犯罪組織　　deportation：強制国外退去（強制送還）　　authority：権限　　drug trafficker：麻薬密売人
halt：…を中止させる

 本文音声

1. Which of the routes below do (1)many illegal immigrants to the U.S. take? （7点）

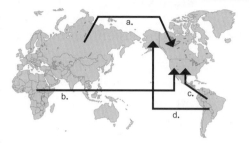

2. According to the text, which of the following is true about (2)the Dream Act? 知識・技能 （7点）
   a. Despite having some opponents, it created a way for young illegal immigrants to get U.S. citizenship.
   b. It enabled young immigrants to get U.S. citizenship because they were productive members of American society.
   c. It was once drafted but has so far not become the law.
   d. When Donald Trump became president, it was halted.

3. Under (3)the Deferred Action for Childhood Arrivals (DACA) program, Dreamers ☐ . (You may choose more than one option.) 段落構成 （完答7点）
   a. are not easily kicked out of the U.S.
   b. can get permission to stay and work in the U.S. for a couple of years
   c. can leave the U.S. if necessary but cannot enter again
   d. cannot enter the U.S. unless they become legal residents

4. Why do opponents to the Dream Act say that (4)Dreamers should be forced back to their home countries? Explain in Japanese. 段落構成 （8点）

_____

_____

5. In the chart below, indicate whether Barack Obama, Donald Trump and Joe Biden are for or against allowing Dreamers to stay in the U.S., and explain their *policies on them in brief Japanese.　policy：政策　情報整理

Presidents	For or Against (各3点)	Policies (各4点)
Barack Obama		
Donald Trump		
Joe Biden		

Lesson

4

語数(速読目標時間)	関連教科	関連SDGs	得 点
397(4分)			
制限時間	公民	8 DECENT WORK AND ECONOMIC GROWTH	
20分			/ 50

1 (1)Laissez-faire is a French term meaning let do or let make. Basically, it means a system in which the government does not try to control business or trade. (2)Under such a system, a country has what is often called a "free market." People buy and sell goods and services freely, both within the country and with other countries. Also, in
5 free markets there are no special laws to control the activities of people or businesses.

2 Actually, there are no countries with Laissez-faire systems today. Many countries have what is referred to as a "free market," but there is always some degree of government control. Laissez-faire is seemingly an ideal situation for both businesses and consumers. (3)Why don't countries adopt this system?

10 **3** The first main reason is to prevent monopolies. A monopoly is when one company becomes so powerful that it controls a product or part of life entirely. This is usually bad for everyone, especially the (4)general public. A company with a monopoly can charge any price for its goods or services, even unfair prices. It may also provide poor service because its customers will not have any other choices. When a monopoly
15 develops, the government often steps in and forces the company to divide into smaller companies.

4 Another big problem is workers' rights. Without government control, workers can be treated very badly. Maybe a company would make employees work 12-hour days and 7-day weeks for very little money. Or, a company might not give employees any
20 health insurance, or might fire employees without reason.

5 Nowadays, most countries have laws that companies must treat their workers well. They must give them 8-hour days, some vacation time, and health insurance. Also, they must have a reason for firing employees.

6 There is one place that came very close to a laissez-faire system — Hong Kong
25 under British rule. In the 1970s, businesses operated according to *market fundamentalism. In such an open economy, it was difficult to predict market trends, and *interference in the market, such as planning how resources should be shared among businesses, was both pointless and harmful. However, the government was responsible for providing public infrastructure such as telecommunications and
30 transportation, and for avoiding market failures. On that point, (5)the laissez-faire in Hong Kong was also a virtual one. However, people who support such a system say that this unique market was the reason for Hong Kong's success.

本文音声

1. Which of the following best describes the author's attitude toward (1)laissez-faire? 🔖主題 （7点）
   a. It is a favorable situation for both companies and consumers.
   b. It is the worst possible situation that people must avoid at all costs.
   c. It is too high an ideal to realize.
   d. It may work, but sometimes it can be dangerous.

2. Translate the following into Japanese: (2)Under such a system, a country has what is often called a "free market." Be sure to make "such a system" clear. 🔖知識・技能 （7点）

_____

_____

3. (3)Why don't countries adopt this system? Give two reasons in Japanese. 🔖文章展開 （各7点）
   • _____
   • _____

4. What word is the closest in meaning to the (4)general public? Answer with a single English word in the text. 🔖段落構成 （7点）

_____

5. Why did the author say that (5)the laissez-faire in Hong Kong was also a virtual one? Explain in detail in Japanese. 🔖段落構成 （8点）

_____

_____

6. According to the text, which of the following is true? 🔖概要理解 （7点）
   a. In Hong Kong in the 1970s, the government didn't step into the market because businesses protested.
   b. Many governments think a monopoly is an unfavorable situation.
   c. Proper working hours, vacations and health insurance are provided under a laissez-faire system.
   d. The terms laissez-faire and free market are used with the same meaning.

1 The treatment of gender varies from language to language. In English, for example, the *third-person pronouns include the *masculine pronoun "he" and the *feminine pronoun "she." The use of these pronouns makes the reader aware of the gender of the characters in any text.

5 **2** In Japanese, however, (1)the *counterpart to "she" did not exist until the 19th century. Until then, there were no gender-distinct third-person pronouns in Japanese. In the Meiji era, Japan underwent rapid westernization, and there was a growing demand for translating Western books. As there was no Japanese *equivalent for "she," "onna" was added to "kare" to create "kanojo."

10 **3** On the other hand, in Japanese, there are many expressions that characteristically show the speaker's gender in various parts of the spoken language. For example, the *final particle "dawa," which means "I mean …" is an expression characteristic of female speakers. In general, women tend to speak politely while men use more (2)blunt expressions. Differences in tone and expression according to gender are probably a 15 more outstanding feature in Japanese language than in English, where the same expressions are typically used regardless of gender.

4 As we have seen, in Western languages the gender distinction is made by pronouns referring to characters, whereas in Japanese it seems that gender has been emphasized by the choice of expression. However, there is a growing voice that does not approve 20 of language making gender distinctions. In particular, words that are *evocative of a particular gender are being replaced by gender-neutral alternatives. For example, "policeman" is now usually referred to as "police officer." Furthermore, in Japanese, there has been less pressure to enforce the use of gender-specific expressions, such as requiring women to speak politely.

25 **5** (3)This trend could represent an adjustment of our language towards a society in which there is no distinction between men and women. Language has been changing according to the demands of the times. More recently, the gender-neutral third-person pronoun (4)"they" has emerged to refer to individuals who are not identified as male or female. Grammatically, "they" is used in the same way as a *plural pronoun, but it can 30 refer to a *singular person. These changes may be challenging to adapt to at first, but having knowledge of them will undoubtedly lead to better linguistic communication.

third-person pronoun：三人称の代名詞　　masculine pronoun：男性代名詞　　feminine pronoun：女性代名詞
counterpart：相当するもの　　equivalent：相当するもの　　final particle：終助詞
evocative：呼び起こす，思い出させる　　plural：複数形の　　singular：単数形の

 本文音声

1. Why was (1)the counterpart to "she" in Japanese generated? Explain in Japanese.

段落構成（7点）

_____

_____

2. The word "(2)blunt" is closest in meaning to ☐. 　　　　　　未知語（7点）
　a. cheerful
　b. kind
　c. strict
　d. unfriendly

3. According to the text, what are the different characteristics of English and Japanese that have been used to emphasize gender distinction? Answer in English.　　文章展開（各7点）
English: _____
Japanese: _____

4. Translate the following into Japanese: (3)This trend could represent an adjustment of our language towards a society in which there is no distinction between men and women. Be sure to make "This trend" clear.　　　　　指示語　　知識・技能（7点）

_____

_____

5-1. How has the use of (4)"they" been changing? Explain it in Japanese.　　段落構成（7点）

_____

_____

5-2. With (4)"they", how can we correct the sentence below? Write the corrected sentence in English.　　　　　　応用（8点）
Everyone can come to our party if he or she wants to come.

_____

Lesson

6

語数（速読目標時間）	関連教科	関連SDGs	得 点
377（3分45秒）	地理歴史	 16 PEACE, JUSTICE AND STRONG INSTITUTIONS	
制限時間			
20分			/ 50

1 There is a (1)famous black-and-white photograph from the so-called period of "*the Third Reich," the rule of Germany under Adolf Hitler. It was taken in Hamburg, Germany, in 1936. The picture is of the workers of a ship building factory, a hundred or more, facing the same direction in the light of the sun. They are stretching out their
5　arms in a *uniform way eagerly *saluting Hitler, their political leader. If you look closely, you can see a man in the upper right who is different from the other workers. His face is gentle but firm. He is surrounded by fellow citizens who have been influenced by the false teachings of the Nazis. He keeps his arms folded across his chest, while the others stretch out their arms. He alone is refusing to show respect to
10　the national leader.

2 Looking back from our perspective, he is the only person in the entire scene who is on the right side of history. Everyone around him is sadly and completely wrong. In that moment, only he could see it. His name is believed to have been August Landmesser. At the time, (2)he could not have known the amount of violence which the
15　enthusiasm of the people around him would lead to. But he had already seen enough to refuse it.

3 Landmesser had joined the Nazi Party himself years before. By (3)now though, he knew clearly that the Nazis were telling Germans lies about Jews and that the party had caused fear, pain, and division even during this early period of their rule. (4)He
20　knew that Jews were anything but "Less-Than-Human." He knew that they were the same citizens, as human as anyone else. In fact, he was in love with a Jewish woman. However, laws had recently been introduced that made their relationship illegal. (5)They were banned from marrying or raising a family, either of which led to what the Nazis regarded as a "racial crime."

25　**4** His personal experience and close connection to the Jewish people allowed him to see beyond the lies easily *embraced by the majority of people. He could see what his fellow citizens chose not to see. In the age of Hitler's rule, it was an act of courage to stand firm against the *tide.

---

the Third Reich：第三帝国　　uniform：一定の，一様の　　salute：敬礼する　　embrace：…を熱心に受け入れる
tide：時流，潮流

 本文音声

1. Which of the following is the (1)famous black-and-white photograph?　　🔖描写 (8点)

a. 　　　　　　b. 　　　　　　c. 　　　　　　d.

2. Translate the following into Japanese: (2)he could not have known the amount of violence which the enthusiasm of the people around him would lead to.　　🔖知識・技能 (9点)

_____

_____

3. What time does (3)now refer to? Explain in Japanese.　　🔖文章展開 (9点)

_____

4. (4)He knew that Jews were anything but "Less-Than-Human" is similar in meaning to ☐.

🔖段落構成 (7点)

a. he knew that Jews were greater than other people

b. he knew that Jews were inferior to non-Jews

c. he knew that Jews were "Less-Than-Human"

d. he knew that Jews were the same as other citizens

5. Translate the following into Japanese: (5)They were banned from marrying or raising a family, either of which led to what the Nazis regarded as a "racial crime."　　🔖知識・技能 (9点)

_____

_____

6. One **fact** from the passage is that ☐.　　🔖事実と意見 (8点)

a. Adolf Hitler visited a ship building factory in Hamburg in 1936

b. everyone around the person with folded arms is sadly and completely wrong

c. in the age of Hitler's rule, it was an act of courage to stand firm against the tide

d. the teachings of the Nazis were false

Lesson

7

語数（速読目標時間）	関連教科	関連SDGs	得 点
407(4分)	家庭	2 ZERO HUNGER	
制限時間			
20分			/ 50

1 We consume meat on a daily basis, but the production of beef, pork, and chicken comes with significant economic and environmental costs. To produce these meats, large numbers of animals must be raised and killed, which consumes a lot of resources. However, a new concept called "(1)cultured meat" is being developed to *alleviate this
5 problem.

2 Cultured meat is produced by taking cells from animals and culturing them in a small space such as a laboratory. Unlike *conventional meat production, it does not require large areas of land, or large amounts of water and grain. Therefore, cultured meat has (2)several major advantages over conventional meat production.

10 **3** First, the process of cultured meat production does not require large numbers of livestock, and thus it reduces the environmental impact. In addition, the more efficient use of the earth's resources is said to contribute not only to environmental problems but also to solving the problem of hunger. In developing countries in particular, the demand for meat continues to increase, and it is difficult to meet this demand through
15 the conventional livestock industry alone. Second, there is also no need for *slaughtering animals, which is a major ethical concern in conventional meat production. People want to eat meat, but few want to kill animals. These sustainability benefits of cultured meat have gained a lot of support and the market is expected to expand rapidly.

20 **4** While the production of cultured meat is already technically *feasible, (3)it has yet to become a mainstream product in the market. One of the reasons for this is the high economic costs of production, such as the expensive culture *fluid required to produce cultured meat. This makes the distribution price of cultured meat much more expensive than that of conventional meat. Further technological advances will be
25 needed to enable mass production and lower prices. Another reason is the psychological hurdle of "safety" and "taste" that consumers face when it comes to accepting cultured meat as an (4)equivalent to conventional meat. It will take time for consumers to perceive cultured meat as an acceptable alternative to conventional meat. Additionally, resistance from existing livestock producers will be inevitable. In
30 the USA, they are already *lobbying the authorities to prevent cultured meat from being labelled as "meat" when sold.

5 Despite these challenges, there are certainly high hopes that cultured meat will help realize more (5)sustainable food production. It may not be long before cultured meat becomes a *viable option for new diets.

本文音声

alleviate：…を軽減する　　conventional：従来の　　slaughter：…を屠殺する　　feasible：実現可能な　　fluid：液体
lobby ... to ～：…に～するよう陳情する，働きかける　　viable：実現可能な

1. Which of the following is true about the (1)cultured meat?　　　　　　　　🔖主題 (6点)

  a. It is made in culture fluid.

  b. It is meat for people whose religion prohibits them from eating ordinary meat.

  c. It is plant-based meat, but tastes just like ordinary meat.

  d. It is taken from animal bodies by a conventional method.

2. What are the (2)several major advantages of cultured meat?　Explain two of them in Japanese.　　　　　　　　　　　　　　　🔖文章展開 (各5点)

  ・ _____

  ・ _____

3. Translate the following into Japanese: (3)it has yet to become a mainstream product in the market.　Be sure to make "it" clear.　　　　　　🔖知識・技能 (7点)

  _____

4. Why can we hardly find any cultured meat in the market?　Give three reasons in Japanese.　　　　　　　　　　　　　　　　🔖段落構成 (各5点)

  ・ _____

  ・ _____

  ・ _____

5. What word has the same meaning as (4)equivalent?　Answer in one English word in the text.　　　　　　　　　　　　　　　🔖知識・技能 (6点)

  _____

6. Cultured meat will help realize more (5)sustainable food production in that ⬚.　　　　　　　　　　　　　　　　　　🔖まとめの段落 (6点)

  a. all starving people will be able to get enough nutrition from it

  b. it will increase the number of people who won't eat meat

  c. its higher price will help producers get more income

  d. fewer livestock will produce less CO_2

Lesson

8

語数（速読目標時間）	関連教科	関連SDGs	得 点
384（3分50秒）	—	3 GOOD HEALTH AND WELL-BEING 11 SUSTAINABLE CITIES AND COMMUNITIES	
制限時間			
20分			/ 50

1 (1)Many of us know first-hand how the spread of infectious diseases can change societal values and lifestyles. It is not a matter of course to remain healthy, and in fact, it is now a well-known fact that great efforts are needed to protect our health. (2)While it is often assumed that maintaining good health requires individual effort and
5 commitment, and this is certainly true, the role of government is just as important.

2 There was once a disease called the plague that drove the whole world into a fear of death. It was an infectious disease spread by rats that bred in unsanitary city conditions. When the city governments realized how serious it was, they built *sewerage systems and kept the cities hygienic in order to control the breeding of rats
10 and prevent plague outbreaks. From this example, you can see that protecting people's health has a lot to do with town development.

3 (3)The role that town development can play in maintaining people's health is not limited to the fight against infectious diseases. Rather, developed countries that have been able to create clean and hygienic towns are increasingly placing more emphasis
15 on combating lifestyle-related diseases. This includes not only direct measures such as providing people with opportunities for regular health check-ups, but also town development that encourages people to unconsciously choose behaviors that help them stay away from the diseases. For example, data show that people who live near (4)parks exercise 1.2 times more frequently than those who do not. Areas which
20 provide more people with access to parks are likely to contribute to the exercise habits of their residents. Furthermore, the positive role of parks in mental health should also not be forgotten, as they promote interaction between people.

4 Likewise, pollution control is a fundamental role of city government. Among all kinds of pollutants, noise from traffic is one of the most often *overlooked. (5)Airplane
25 noise in particular is the most significant, and some studies have shown that the average blood pressure of people living near airports is higher than that of people who do not. As you know, high blood pressure can lead to heart-related illnesses. From the point of view of healthy town development, measures such as greening the area around airports and soundproofing the houses in the *vicinity would be effective.

---

sewerage system：下水道システム　　overlook：…を見落とす　　vicinity：近辺，周辺

本文音声

1. Which of the following is an example of (1)many of us knowing first-hand how the spread of infectious diseases can change societal values and lifestyles? ⌐ 応用 (8点)

   a. AI technology enables cars to drive themselves automatically.

   b. Emperor Shomu, wishing to eradicate smallpox, built the great Buddha statue in Nara.

   c. Many schools allowed students to attend classes at home during the COVID-19 pandemic.

   d. When tuberculosis spread during the Industrial Revolution, many workers set up unions and protested against their poor working conditions.

2. Translate the following into Japanese: (2)While it is often assumed that maintaining good health requires individual effort and commitment, and this is certainly true, the role of government is just as important. ⌐ 知識・技能 (11点)

   _____

   _____

3. In paragraph 3, (3)the role that town development can play in maintaining people's health is not limited to the fight against infectious diseases means ☐. ⌐ 段落構成 (8点)

   a. towns as well as other groups fight against infectious diseases

   b. towns not only fight against infectious diseases, but also against other kind of diseases

   c. towns not only fight against infectious diseases, but also help patients recover

   d. towns play a role in maintaining people's health and other aspects of their lives

4. How do (4)parks contribute to people's health? Explain two merits in Japanese. ⌐ 段落構成 (各7点)

   · _____

   · _____

5. Which is **not** true about the (5)airplane noise? ⌐ 論理 (9点)

   a. Airplanes which emit less noise were developed.

   b. People exposed to it are likely to suffer heart-related illnesses.

   c. Soundproofing the houses is a good way to decrease it.

   d. Trees around airports can decrease it.

語数（速読目標時間）	関連教科	関連SDGs	得 点
406（4分）	地理歴史・情報	—	
制限時間			
20分			/ 50

1 As we put ever more of our lives on storage devices like external drives, tablets, and smartphones, we place bits and pieces of our culture there as well: music, art, literature, maps, videos, and photos. These are all *artifacts of our culture. However, there are problems with this method of storage. If these storage methods become
5 outdated in the future, the stored data may become inaccessible, just as we struggle to access the contents of *floppy disks now. And if you think that keeping it all in the Cloud is the answer, it isn't. Take *a solar flare as an example. If a major solar flare wipes out Amazon, Apple, Facebook, and other data centers, all will be lost. Or, if one of these companies goes bankrupt, it is possible that the data it hosts will be lost. The
10 point is that there are many ways that we could lose our digital culture.

2 Such a loss of our digital culture could make it difficult for people in the future to understand how we lived. This is because (1)we barely think about the small bits and pieces of a culture that often deliver the greatest clues and insights to *archeologists and *anthropologists studying past cultures. The materials and process used to make
15 (2)an ancient clay pot, for example, tell us about the food culture of the society that made it. (2)The layout of buildings can tell us if the society was ruled by a king or queen or if it was more *communal. Studying humanity's past helps us navigate today and seek to understand the future. Through archeology and anthropology, we have been able to understand different political systems and methods of governance in the past
20 which have informed how we govern our societies today.

3 In the distant future, we may seek to understand at what point and how artificial intelligence came to dominate in our societies and how it affected our cultures. We may want to know how we let social media *run amok and what impacts, good and bad, it has had on cultures around the world. Culture is the knowledge we use to
25 navigate our life and world.

4 The question then becomes this: How do we ensure that our digital lives are preserved as much as possible? How do they get copied into new storage formats? (3)Preserving our present for the future is critical for cultural understanding and navigating our world in the future.

---

artifact：人工遺物　　floppy disk：フロッピーディスク（記憶媒体の一つ。現代ではほとんど使われていない。）
a solar flare：太陽フレア（太陽で不定期に起こる爆発的な増光現象）　　archeologist：考古学者　　anthropologist：人類学者
communal：共同的な　　run amok：暴走する

本文音声

1. The author wrote this text in order to ☐.
   a. emphasize the importance of accepting new technologies
   b. help people in the distant future look into our current life
   c. let people know how fun it is to learn about ancient lives
   d. make people aware of how often data disappears by accident

2. Translate the following into Japanese: (1)we barely think about the small bits and pieces of a culture that often deliver the greatest clues and insights to archeologists and anthropologists studying past cultures. 知識・技能 (9点)

_____

_____

3. Complete the English sentence below about (2)an ancient clay pot and (2)the layout of buildings. 知識・技能 論理 (完答7点)
   An ancient clay pot and the layout of buildings are to people living today what
   (   ) (   ) are to people in the future.

4-1. For (3)preserving our present for the future, what should we do? Answer in English. 段落構成 (10点)

   We should _____

4-2. Why has the task of (3)preserving our present for the future not yet been completed? Explain in detail in Japanese. 文章展開 (10点)

_____

_____

5. Which of the following does **not** match the author's opinion? 筆者の意見 (7点)
   a. Archeology and anthropology may inform us of how we should govern today's societies.
   b. Floppy disks are outdated and hardly used now.
   c. Social media has both positive and negative aspects.
   d. We should be careful about accepting AI in our current society.

1 Cargo ships release large amounts of carbon dioxide (CO_2) into the atmosphere. (1)Efforts are being made to convert the power source of these cargo ships from fossil fuels to wind power. Imagine that the cup of coffee in your hand was transported all the way from Colombia not on a giant polluting container ship, but by a strong sailing
5 ship that only uses wind power. That is the vision of TransOceanic Wind Transport (TOWT), a small cargo company based in France which is now working on transporting tens of thousands of tons of cargo per year.

2 TOWT was established in 2011 and has already transported over 1,000 tons of cargo across the ocean using small sailing ships. Now, the company is constructing
10 four larger sailing ships which will travel along four ocean routes between Europe and destinations including New York, Guadeloupe, Brazil and the Ivory Coast. Each ship will be able to carry 1,100 tons of cargo. The ships will have large sails and diesel engines that can be used only when necessary. According to TOWT, these sailing ships will reduce emissions by 90 percent compared to (2)conventional cargo ships.

15 **3** Every year, the conventional shipping industry emits around 600 to 700 million tons of CO_2 into the atmosphere. This is roughly the same amount of CO_2 that Germany produces, and it is about 2-3 percent of global CO_2 emissions. However, (3)it is difficult to reduce carbon emissions in the shipping industry. Electric engines are not powerful enough to get ships across oceans. Furthermore, there are not enough
20 alternative fuels such as hydrogen or biofuels to power ships.

4 TOWT already has orders worth over 100 million euros from 30 companies that want to transport various goods from cocoa and coffee to wine and champagne. These companies are willing to pay extra to be able to tell their customers that their products arrived by a low-carbon ship.

25 **5** TOWT is not the only company building larger sailing cargo ships. (4)SAILCARGO INC., a company in Costa Rica, is close to finishing its first wooden sailing ship. In the future, the ship will carry around 250 tons of cargo between North and South America using only wind power and an electric engine.

6 "Wind should play a major role in reducing carbon emissions in the shipping
30 industry," says Aoife O'Leary, director of international shipping at the non-profit organization, Environmental Defense Fund. "For every kilometer you can sail with wind, you're saving yourself from spending money on a very expensive alternative fuel."

本文音声

1. Translate the following into Japanese: (1)Efforts are being made to convert the power source of these cargo ships from fossil fuels to wind power. Be sure to make "these cargo ships" clear.

_____

_____

2. What are (2)conventional cargo ships? Answer in English from the text.

文章展開 (8点)

_____

3. Why (3)is it difficult to reduce carbon emissions in the shipping industry? Explain in Japanese.

段落構成 (9点)

_____

_____

4. Why has TOWT been successful in getting many orders from other companies? Explain in Japanese.

論理 (9点)

_____

_____

5. Which of the following is likely to be the biggest advantage of (4)SAILCARGO INC.'s ship over TOWT's ship?

論理 (8点)

a. It is made of more eco-friendly materials.

b. It will be able to carry more cargo in one voyage.

c. It will go faster.

d. It will travel different ocean routes.

6. Which of the following are true according to the text? Choose **two** options. The order does not matter.

全体把握 (完答8点)

a. Sailing ships will produce only 90% of the emissions of conventional cargo ships.

b. Shipping items by sailing ships costs more than by conventional cargo ships.

c. The shipping industry in Germany is responsible for about 2-3 percent of global CO_2 emissions.

d. TOWT owns ships which can carry up to 1,000 tons of cargo.

e. Wind power seems to be a very cost-effective alternative fuel for cargo ships.

1　The effects of videogames are a long-running topic that is often controversial in the fields of education and psychology.　Recent studies on students of all ages have shown a strong correlation between the time they spend playing video games and their grades in school.　In short, the studies have revealed (1)several negative impacts of
5　playing videogames for long hours per day on students' behavior and performance, such as: (a) unsatisfactory results in school, (b) aggressive behaviors, (c) shorter sleeping hours, and (d) addiction to gaming.

2　One private university conducted a survey about the effects of videogames on students' well-being and performances.　In January 2023, there was an interesting
10　presentation given at a world-wide educational conference.　The 20-minute presentation reported the analysis of the questionnaires collected from 3,600 students studying at the institution.

Table 1. Groups of Students Divided by the Hours of Playing Videogames

Hours	*3 hours or more*	*1 to 2 hours*	*0 hours*
Percentages	40%	50%	10%
Groups	(Group A)	(Group B)	(Group C)

As shown in Table 1, the participants were divided into three groups based on the number of hours they played various videogames per day.　Ninety percent of the
15　students played videogames daily.　The presenter added some important details in the talk.　Those in Group A usually played videogames anytime outside the classroom whenever they liked.　Incredibly, only ten percent of them claimed videogaming was a source of trouble despite the fact that they stayed up very late to play games although having classes the next day.　On the other hand, one common feature in Group B was
20　that they successfully limited their time for gaming, such as only during their commuting, or just an hour or two per day as a brief leisure activity.

3　The presentation also dealt with students' self-evaluation of their daily behaviors.　Interestingly, the survey showed some results that contradicted (2)the expectations of the researchers.　As in Table 2 below, the most important key for assessing the effects
25　of the games on students' (3)well-being did not simply come from whether or not they played videogames, but how well they could regulate themselves.　Borrowing a presenter's words, "there seem to be many negative aspects of students' behavior that do not necessarily stem from playing videogames."

Table 2. Percentage of Positive Responses in Students' Self-evaluations (The percentage indicates the number of those who answered "yes" to each question.)

Daily Behavior	Completing homework in time	Getting enough sleep	Doing physical exercise daily	Keeping in touch with friends in real life	Managing anger
Group A	12%	2%	12%	38%	72%
Group B	76%	65%	36%	86%	78%
Group C	69%	39%	35%	82%	71%

本文音声

1. What are the (1)several negative impacts of playing videogames for long hours per day? Explain in Japanese. 　　　　　　　　　　　　　　　　　　　　　　　　　　　⌐ 知識・技能 （9点）

_____

_____

2. According to paragraph 2, one **opinion** about the presentation is that ⬜. ⌐ 事実と意見 （7点）
   a. 10% of the students who answered the questionnaire play no videogames
   b. 3,600 students studying at a private university were asked to answer the questionnaire
   c. it was incredible that few heavy-gamers regarded videogaming as the source of their trouble
   d. people who play videogames for a few hours a day tend to limit their gaming time

3. What is likely to be (2)the expectations of the researchers? Explain in Japanese.
   　　　　　　　　　　　　　　　　　　　　　　　　　　　　　　　　⌐ 文章展開 （10点）

_____

_____

4-1. According to Table 2, which group can be said to have had the highest level of (3)well-being? 　　　　　　　　　　　　　　　　　　　　　　　⌐ 表の読み取り （6点）
   a. Group A 　　　　b. Group B 　　　　c. Group C

4-2. The most appropriate reason why the survey result was as in Question 4-1 is that ⬜.
   　　　　　　　　　　　　　　　　　　　　　　　　　　　　　　　　⌐ 論理 （10点）

   a. the amount of time spent on games did not directly affect the students' well-being
   b. the more time the students spent on games, the lower their well-being got
   c. the students were happier playing games in moderation than not at all
   d. the students' self-regulation led to higher levels of well-being

5. Choose what **cannot** be seen from the two tables alone. You may choose more than one option. 　　　　　　　　　　　　　　　　　　　⌐ 全体把握 （完答8点）
   a. Heavy gamers usually played videogames outside the classroom whenever they liked.
   b. Many students who didn't play videogames suffered from a lack of sleep.
   c. Ninety percent of the students played videogames daily.
   d. Only ten percent of the students claimed videogaming was a source of trouble despite the fact that they stayed up very late to play games although having classes the next day.

Lesson

12

語数（速読目標時間）	関連教科	関連SDGs	得　点
491（4分55秒）	理科	 9 INDUSTRY, INNOVATION AND INFRASTRUCTURE	
制限時間			
20分			/ 50

1 Walking through a forest, you may have a chance to see a spider's web. It is one of nature's more common occurrences. There are many different types of spider webs, but perhaps the most common is (1)the orb web, or a web that is a series of wheel-shaped, *concentric outlines with silk threads going out from the center of the web. Spiders, just like humans, work at different speeds and each spider makes a unique web. It takes about 30 minutes to one hour for most spiders to construct an *elaborate web of silk thread. These webs are not homes for the spiders, but they are used as traps to catch other insects so the spiders can eat.

2 Spider webs are interesting not only for their shape and for their use, but also because of the silk that the spiders produce. For over one hundred years, engineers and scientists have been trying to reproduce the spider's silk because (2)it is quite amazing. Spider silk is one of the strongest materials known to mankind.

3 It is stronger than the toughest steel but at the same time incredibly light. Not only is it strong and light, but it is also very *elastic. It can stretch up to 140% of its original length. Another amazing thing about spider silk is that, when the silk is pulled, it becomes very soft and then it *stiffens again quickly.

4 This makes the silk and the spider's web very *resilient and strong. Due to this resilience and strength, insects can't escape a web once they are caught in it. Also, (3)a web will not break easily when someone tries to brush it away, nor will it break easily in strong winds. Even if a place in the web becomes weakened due to a break in one of the silk strings, the web will still function as intended.

5 These properties of a spider's silk are so important that scientists and engineers alike realize that there are many possible applications for such a product in areas as diverse as heavy industry, the military, space and deep-sea exploration, medicine and even more. Unfortunately, such silk cannot be "(4)farmed" naturally, as spiders will fight to the death when put together in groups.

6 Because there are so many applications for such a strong material, scientists and engineers have been trying for many years to reproduce the silk artificially. If a company can succeed in doing so, it will no doubt obtain enormous financial profits. Unfortunately, (5)research so far has yet to *yield successful results. While some chemists are focusing on reproducing the superb strength of spider silk, others are trying to figure out how spider silk can be so light and flexible. These two seemingly opposite qualities have challenged scientists in their attempts to reproduce it. While efforts to do so will no doubt continue, it's too bad scientists cannot approach the

35 problem more directly, simply by asking spiders how they do it.

concentric：同心の（同じ中心をもった）　　elaborate：精巧な　　elastic：伸縮性のある　　stiffen：硬くなる
resilient：弾力性のある　　yield：…を生み出す

1. Which best describes (1)the orb web?　　　　　　　　　　　　　　　◔知識・技能　◔描写 （7点）

a. 　　　　　　　　b. 　　　　　　　　c. 　　　　　　　　d.

2. Why does the author say (2)it is quite amazing?　Explain in 50-70 words in Japanese.

◔文章展開 （10点）

				50														
	70																	

3. Translate the following into Japanese: (3)a web will not break easily when someone tries to brush it away, nor will it break easily in strong winds.　　　◔知識・技能 （8点）

_____

_____

4. (4)Farmed can be replaced with ☐.　　　　　　　　　　　　◔修辞 （8点）
   a. found　　　b. produced　　　c. socialized　　　d. succeeded

5. Why has (5)research so far yet to yield successful results?　Explain in Japanese.　◔段落構成 （10点）

_____

_____

6. Which of the following is true about the spider web?　　　　　　◔内容理解 （7点）
   a. As it is called "クモの巣" in Japanese, spiders use it as their homes.
   b. In spite of challenges, scientists will continue to work on reproducing it.
   c. It costs as much as true silk and its high price prevents it from coming onto the market.
   d. It has yet to be reproduced successfully because it takes spiders as long as 30 minutes to one hour to construct an elaborate web of silk thread.

Lesson

13

語数（速読目標時間）	関連教科	関連SDGs	得　点
472（4分40秒）	理科	 15 LIFE ON LAND	
制限時間			
20分			/ 50

1 One reason that many of us fail to understand trees is that they live on a different time scale than we do. There are trees that are more than 9,500 years old, which is 115 times longer than the average human lifetime. ₍₁₎<u>Living things with such a luxury of time on their hands</u> can afford to take things at a relaxed pace. The electrical impulses that pass through the roots of trees, for example, move at the slow rate of one third of an inch per second. But why, you might ask, do trees pass electrical impulses through their roots at all?

2 The answer is that trees need to communicate, and electrical impulses are just one of their many ways of doing so. Trees also use the senses of smell and taste for communication. If a long-necked giraffe starts eating a tree called an African acacia, the tree releases a chemical into the air which signals that a threat is at hand. As the chemical drifts through the air and reaches other trees, they "smell" it and are warned of the danger. Even before the giraffe reaches them, they begin producing toxic chemicals. Likewise, the *saliva of leaf-eating insects can be "tasted" by the leaf being eaten. In response, the tree sends out a chemical signal that attracts predators that feed on that particular leaf-eating insect. ₍₂₎<u>Life in the slow lane is not always dull</u>.

3 But the most remarkable thing about trees is how social they are. The trees in a forest look after each other, ₍₃₎<u>even going so far as to feed the *stump of a tree that has been cut down with sugars and other nutrients</u>, and so keep it alive for sometimes hundreds of years. Only some stumps survive in this way, and perhaps they are the parents of the trees that make up the forest today. A tree's most important means of staying connected to other trees is a "Wood Wide Web" of soil *fungi that connects vegetation in an intimate network that enables the sharing of an enormous amount of information and other necessities. ₍₄₎<u>Scientific research aimed at understanding the remarkable abilities of this partnership between fungi and plants has only just begun</u>.

4 The reason trees share food and communicate is that they need each other. It requires a forest to create an ecosystem suitable for sustainable tree growth, and it's not surprising, therefore, that trees living by themselves have far shorter lives than those living connected together in forests. Perhaps the saddest plants of all are those we have allowed to become trapped in our agricultural systems; ₍₅₎<u>they live out their lives in silence, quite unable to communicate with others</u>. Farmers should learn from the forests and ₍₆₎<u>cultivate a little more wildness among their grain and potatoes</u> so that they too will start "talking" with their neighbors.

saliva：唾液　　stump：切り株　　fungi：菌（類）〔複数形扱い〕

1. What are the (1)living things with such a luxury of time on their hands? Answer in English.

言いかえ表現（9点）

_____

2. Why can the author say that (2)life in the slow lane is not always dull? Explain in about 60 letters in Japanese.

まとめの文（10点）

											60								

3. Which of the following is the closest in meaning to (3)even going so far as to feed the stump of a tree that has been cut down with sugars and other nutrients?　知識・技能（7点）

　a. A tree can change other trees into stumps with sugars and other nutrients it contains.

　b. A tree can provide stumps with sugars and other nutrients it contains.

　c. A tree can send its sugars and other nutrients to stumps that are located far away.

　d. If we go deep into a forest, we can find stumps covered with sugars and other nutrients.

4. Which of the following is the closest in meaning to (4)scientific research aimed at understanding the remarkable abilities of this partnership between fungi and plants has only just begun?　知識・技能　段落構成（7点）

　a. Scientists are trying to find out which fungi make the recently identified plant.

　b. Scientists have recently understood how fungi become larger plants.

　c. Scientists tried to understand what role fungi had just begun to play in forests.

　d. Until recently, scientists have not studied the role that fungi have played in forests.

5. Translate the following into Japanese: (5)they live out their lives in silence, quite unable to communicate with others. Be sure to make "they" clear.　知識・技能（10点）

_____

_____

6. Which of the following methods is the closest to (6)cultivating a little more wildness among their grain and potatoes?　応用（7点）

　a. Getting rid of small potatoes so that bigger ones can grow better.

　b. Planting grain and potatoes among other plant species.

　c. Not taking care of grain and potatoes once they have been planted.

　d. Not using chemicals such as pesticides nor fertilizers.

以下の英文は，アメリカの大学を卒業後，短期間インドネシアでホストファミリーの家に滞在しながら，現地の学校で教師として働いた女性の手記です。

1 "'The Ant and the Grasshopper,'" my student Riswanda said, "teaches us that we must help others, even if they have not made the most practical decisions."

2 I gave her (1)a tight smile. I was six months into my year teaching English at an Islamic high school in East Java, Indonesia. Riswanda's class was the seventh I had

5 taught that week, and each had missed (2)the point of this Aesop's *fable. A grasshopper who plays his *fiddle all summer and fails to collect grain for the winter goes hungry, while the *industrious ant family who works hard during the summer months is rewarded with full stomachs. As I lectured on the *virtues of hard work and planning ahead, I saw Riswanda's face *scrunched in confusion.

10 **3** In my second year at Stanford, I took a class on cross-cultural communication. We learned about Geert Hofstede's theory on cultural dimensions, which aims to measure and explain cultural differences. In the *individualism rankings, America scores a 91, the highest in the world. Indonesia scores a 14, one of the lowest.

4 The country's strongly communal culture showed up in every dimension of my life.

15 My host family included two grandmothers, an aunt, three cousins who tried to repair motorcycle parts all day, and their distant and unemployed relatives who moved in and out constantly. I (3)thought about myself a few months before, a Stanford fourth-year student desperately searching for jobs in order not to burden my parents by depending on them for support after graduation.

20 **5** I also saw differences at school. Teachers actually skipped class to visit relatives in the hospital or to drive neighbors to the airport, which would have been unimaginable in my public high school in North Carolina. On test days, my brightest students would share their answers with those who had put in absolutely no effort. It was the perfect example of ants helping grasshoppers, and it seemed *acutely *unjust.

25 **6** Riswanda came up to me after class with her photocopied fable. "Miss, I don't understand," she said. "What's so wrong with playing the fiddle all summer?"

7 Her question has stayed with me. The grasshopper's job was far from practical, but it added beauty to a boring field. The cousins staying in my host family's house didn't contribute financially, but they never failed to brighten my day with their big laughs.

30 Teachers skipped class not because they were lazy, but because they believed that helping others in tough situations was more important than making tired teenagers

本文音声

solve math problems repeatedly. (4)What I perceived as cheating in my classroom could also be seen as a selfless act: lifting up the entire class rather than elevating oneself.

8 I have come to question my own fable: that you can measure people's value by
35 their productivity. As I get back to life in America, I'm bringing with me (5)the wisdom of my students, teachers and housemates — the ants and the grasshoppers alike.

---

fable：寓話，童話   fiddle：バイオリン   industrious：勤勉な   virtue：美徳   scrunch：…をしわくちゃにする
individualism：個人主義，利己主義   acutely：痛切に，ひどく   unjust：不正な

次ページへ続く➡

1. Why did the author gave Riswanda (1)a tight smile? Explain in Japanese. 文章展開 （9点）

_____

_____

2. What did the author think (2)the point of this Aesop's fable was? Answer in an English phrase in paragraph 2. 段落構成 （9点）

_____

3. The author (3)thought about herself a few months before because _____. 知識・技能 （7点）
   a. she had to search for jobs
   b. she looked back on her fun university days, facing her current tough career
   c. she realized how industrious she had been compared to the people in and around her house
   d. she regretted that she had still been depending on her parents for support

4. What was (4)what she perceived as cheating in her classroom like? Explain in Japanese. 文章展開 （9点）

_____

_____

5. What was (5)the wisdom of her students, teachers and housemates? Explain in Japanese. まとめの段落 （9点）

_____

_____

6. Which of the following statements are true? Choose **two** options. The order does not matter. 内容理解 （完答7点）
   a. Riswanda thought that the grasshopper should be saved because unemployment was not a bad thing.
   b. Riswanda was a seventh-grade student.
   c. The host family's three cousins worked as motorcycle repairpersons.
   d. The writer wrote this article in Indonesia.
   e. There were many Indonesian students who couldn't get the original point of "The Ant and the Grasshopper."

1 In recent years, it has become clear that many children around the world are not learning to read proficiently. Even though the majority of children are in school, a large proportion are not acquiring fundamental skills. Moreover, 260 million children are not even in school. This is a serious learning crisis that threatens countries' efforts to achieve the Sustainable Development Goals (SDGs). Without foundational learning, students often fail to succeed later in school or when they join the workforce.

2 New data show that 53% of all children in low- and middle-income countries suffer from (1)learning poverty, which means being unable to read and understand a simple text by age 10. Age 10, when children are expected to be in the fourth grade, is when many children finish mastering "the mechanics" of basic reading. By then, they can interpret most words and start to grow as independent readers.

3 Once children have learned to (2)become fluent readers, they read faster and this enables them to focus on meaning. Faster reading means more practice and, very often, more enjoyment. More reading improves vocabulary and background knowledge, improving overall reading skills. By contrast, if they do not obtain these skills by approximately age 10, they tend to fall further and further behind, and few catch up.

4 If hundreds of millions of children are not getting foundational reading and other skills (3)when they should, what can be done about it? First, it is critical to raise awareness of the problem. One way to do this is to adopt a simple indicator that is easy to understand and track. This is why (4)the learning poverty indicator was introduced. It measures a straightforward concept: What share of children around the world are not able to read and understand a short age-appropriate text by around age 10.

5 Despite the barriers confronting girls in some areas of education, girls have lower rates of learning poverty than boys do. Table 1 shows that girls are, on average, 5 percentage points less learning-poor than boys. The difference is significantly smaller in Europe, Central Asia and North America, and largest in the Middle East, North Africa, East Asia and the Pacific.

次ページへ続く➡

本文音声

Table 1. Learning poverty by gender and subgroups (from a subsample of countries)

		Male (%)	Female (%)
Regions	East Asia & the Pacific	29. 6	21. 1
	Europe & Central Asia	10. 0	8. 2
	The Middle East & North Africa	66. 0	56. 8
	North America	8. 0	7. 1
	Sub-Saharan Africa	86. 4	83. 0
Income	High income	8. 4	6. 6
	Upper-middle income	44. 6	39. 5
	Lower-middle income	55. 1	45. 9
	Low income	93. 3	93. 5
World	All	43. 6	38. 9

Source: Azevedo and others (2019), The Global Learning Assessment Database

6 The gender difference is significantly greater in middle-income countries. While in high-income and low-income countries differences are quite small, the gap reaches 9.2 percentage points in lower-middle-income countries (Table 1).

7 Progress in reducing learning poverty is far too slow. At the current rate of improvement, in 2030 about 43% of children will still be learning-poor. Even if countries reduce their learning poverty at the fastest rates we have seen so far in this century, the goal of ending it will not be attained by 2030.

8 Learning poverty places children's future and the development of their countries at risk. Eliminating learning poverty is an urgent objective, one that is critical to achieving the goals of ending extreme poverty and advancing shared prosperity. It is critical to accelerate (5)efforts now to ensure that children will be able to read by the time they turn 10 years of age.

1. Why is the term (1)learning poverty applied mainly to children under 10?　Explain in Japanese.　　　　　　　　　　　　　　　　　　　✎ 主題 (10点)

_____

_____

2. The author stressed the importance of (2)becoming fluent readers because ⬚.

✎ 段落構成 (7点)

  a. being able to do so provides learners with opportunities to read more texts and improve reading skills

  b. students who can read fast tend to be regarded as excellent learners

  c. too many long texts are given in examinations

  d. when you read a text aloud, people usually like to hear it spoken rapidly

3. What time does (3)when they should refer to?　Explain in Japanese.　　✎ 文章展開 (10点)

_____

_____

4. What is (4)the learning poverty indicator?　Explain in Japanese.　　✎ 知識・技能 (9点)

_____

_____

5. Which is true about table 1?　　　　　　　　　　　　　　　　✎ 読み比べ (7点)

  a. About two thirds of the boys in countries in the Middle East & North Africa are not able to read and understand a short age-appropriate text around age 10.

  b. Countries in Sub-Saharan Africa are suffering the most from poverty.

  c. In countries in Europe & Central Asia, 10% of the boys are illiterate.

  d. Low-income households show the smallest gender gaps in learning poverty.

6. Which of the following kinds of (5)efforts should be accelerated?　　✎ まとめの段落 (7点)

  a. To end extreme poverty and advance shared prosperity.

  b. To introduce the learning poverty indicator into every school.

  c. To help students become fluent readers.

  d. To remove the barriers confronting girls in some areas of education.

Lesson

16

語数（速読目標時間）	関連教科	関連 SDGs	得　点
590（5分55秒）	地理歴史	10 REDUCED INEQUALITIES　16 PEACE, JUSTICE AND STRONG INSTITUTIONS	
制限時間			
20分			/ 50

1 After Columbus returned to Europe and announced his discoveries, Spain quickly sent soldiers and settlers to start colonies in the Americas. One hundred years after Columbus' first voyage, the Spanish had built many towns in South America, Central America, and Mexico. England, however, did not send many people to the New World for a long time after Columbus' discovery. During the sixteenth century, England was often fighting with Spain, so the English were afraid to send their own people to the Americas.

2 Sir Walter Raleigh was a good friend of Queen Elizabeth of England, so the queen let Raleigh start an English colony in North America. Raleigh called the region of the new settlement "Virginia" after the queen. A group of about 100 people from England entered Roanoke Island, near the coast of Virginia and (1)established a base there in 1587.

3 After the Roanoke Colony, the English tried again to start a town in North America. In 1607, they started a colony at Jamestown, on the mainland of Virginia. Businessmen started the Jamestown colony, but some of those who came to the area from England did not want to work very hard; they had hoped to find gold quickly and go home as rich men. Also, there was often trouble with the local Native Americans, who were not very friendly to the strange newcomers.

4 Although (2)Jamestown was not very successful in the beginning, the colony grew little by little. When the English found out about tobacco from the Native Americans, the custom of smoking quickly became popular in Europe. After this, farmers in Virginia made a lot of money growing tobacco and selling it in England. Many Virginia farmers began to use the "plantation system" to grow tobacco and other products such as cotton and sugar. The plantation system used African slaves to do the heavy farm work. Gradually, the plantation system became very important to the economy and way of life of the southern colonies, but never to the northern colonies such as New England. (3)This difference between the North and South later led to the American Civil War, which lasted from 1861 to 1865.

5 The English settlers around Jamestown often fought with the Native Americans who were afraid that the new arrivals would take away their land. (4)Captain John Smith was a brave man who had explored the coast of North America. Once, while Smith was the leader of the Jamestown colony, he was caught by a local Native American chief named Powhatan. Chief Powhatan decided to kill John Smith. But, just then, the

本文音声

chief's daughter arrived. This Native American princess named Pocahontas had visited

35 Jamestown and had become friendly with the English people living there. Pocahontas asked her father, Chief Powhatan, not to kill Captain Smith. Finally, Chief Powhatan let Smith go free and he returned to Jamestown safely.

6 Pocahontas later became a Christian, and she married an Englishman named John Rolfe. Rolfe was the first Englishman to grow tobacco in Virginia. Jamestown and all

40 of Virginia became a profitable colony because people made a lot of money from tobacco. More and more English people came to Virginia to start tobacco farms and plantations.

7 In 1616, John Rolfe, his wife Pocahontas, and several other friendly Native Americans went to England, and Pocahontas met the English king and queen. Sadly,

45 Pocahontas became sick and died just before her return to America. Her husband went back to Virginia, but after Pocahontas' death, the English and the Native Americans began fighting again, and there was no peace for many years.

1. Where did a group of about 100 people from England (1)establish a base in 1587?

文章展開 (7 点)

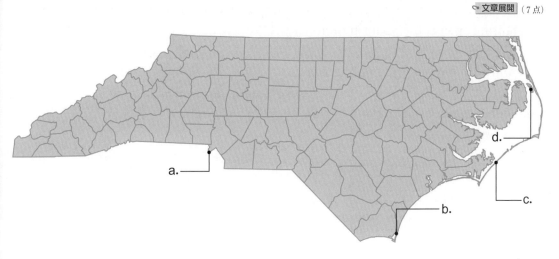

2. Why was (2)Jamestown not very successful in the beginning?　Give two reasons in Japanese.　　　　　　　　　　　　　　　　　　　　　　◇文章展開 (各 7 点)

　・_____

　・_____

3. Translate the following into Japanese: (3)This difference between the North and South later led to the American Civil War, which lasted from 1861 to 1865.　Be sure to make "This difference" clear.　　　　　　　　　　　　　　　　◇知識・技能 (7 点)

　_____

　_____

4. Describe the relationship between (4)Captain John Smith and Pocahontas in detail in Japanese.　　　　　　　　　　　　　　　　　　　　　　　◇段落構成 (8 点)

　_____

　_____

　_____

5. Arrange the following events in the order in which they occurred.　　◇知識・技能 (7 点)
　　a. Chief Powhatan decided to kill John Smith.
　　b. Pocahontas asked her father to let John Smith go free.
　　c. Pocahontas married an Englishman named John Rolfe.
　　d. Pocahontas visited Jamestown and became friendly with the English people living there.
　　(　　) → (　　) → (　　) → (　　)

6. Which of the following is definitely true according to the text?　　　◇論理 (7 点)
　　a. During the 16th century, England sent no people to the Americas for fear of fighting against the Spanish there.
　　b. If Pocahontas had returned to America alive, the English and the Native Americans would not have begun fighting again.
　　c. In the early 17th century, several Native Americans went to Europe.
　　d. Queen Elizabeth of England had another name, "Virginia."

❶ In the *Sichuan region of southwest China, farm workers climb apple trees and use brushes made from chicken feathers to collect *pollen from the flowers of one tree and then shake it onto the flowers of another. Why do the local farmers spend so much valuable time performing a task — (1)<u>pollination</u> — that insects have done for countless
5 generations? The simple answer is that there are no longer enough insects living in the area. As in many places across the world, insect numbers have been steadily decreasing for years. While there are (2)<u>several possible explanations for these worrying declines</u>, they share one common feature — all are related to human activities.

❷ In recent years, it has become clear that, in general, insect populations are falling.
10 However, it is extremely difficult to know exactly the extent to which this is happening. Unlike rhinos, tigers, or elephants, insects are small and not easily counted. In addition, they tend not to be as widely researched. But scientists around the world have reported huge drops in the numbers of insects such as butterflies, beetles, and, most famously, bees. *Entomologists have found that, in recent decades, wild bee
15 numbers have (3)<u>crashed</u> worldwide. Similar shocking figures have been reported for several other species of insects.

❸ Unfortunately, the drop in insect numbers is overwhelmingly the result of human activities. The overuse of chemicals on farms and in our gardens is often *cited as the main cause of the problem. (4)<u>It is the use of these chemicals in Sichuan that has led to
20 the loss of the insects that used to pollinate the apple trees</u>. The loss of wild areas where insects live is also an important factor. Every year, more forests and grasslands are cleared for agriculture or housing; insects are simply losing their homes. In addition, climate change is having a *catastrophic impact on many insect species, which cannot cope with global warming. Studies by entomologists in the rainforests
25 of Costa Rica have shown that higher temperatures have led to the near disappearance of many insect species.

❹ Although there is now little doubt that insect populations are declining, we do not yet know what a world without insects would look like. Perhaps there are even some (5)<u>people who would prefer to live without such "creepy crawlies."</u> However, (6)<u>if insects
30 were to disappear completely, it would have almost unimaginable consequences for life on our planet</u>. It would not only be insects that would *vanish; many birds, small mammals and *reptiles, as well as fish, which all rely on insects as their main food source, would also be wiped out. The loss of insects would have terrible effects for us

次ページへ続く➡

本文音声

humans, too. Without insects to pollinate our crops, it would be impossible to grow
35 enough fruit and vegetables to feed human populations. If we end up having to hand-
pollinate all our crops in the way that is already being done with apples in southwest
China, food prices will soar and, as always, the poorest around the world will suffer
most.

5 The current decline in insect populations has brought about many serious
40 concerns. However, there might still be time to prevent the most severe impacts.
Entomologists have pointed out that the actions that ordinary citizens take can really
make a difference. We should avoid using *insecticides and other chemicals in our
homes and gardens, and grow flowers and other plants that support insects. In
addition, we should purchase organic produce where possible. If we take these
45 measures, we can help (7)our small, struggling six-legged friends, and the whole natural
world can begin to recover.

Sichuan：四川(中国の地名)　　pollen：花粉　　entomologist：昆虫学者　　cite：…を引用する，挙げる
catastrophic：壊滅的な　　vanish：消える　　reptile：爬虫類　　insecticide：殺虫剤

1. What is the meaning of (1)pollination? Answer in Japanese. 未知語の推測 （7点）

_____

2. From the passage, give three examples of (2)several possible explanations for these worrying declines. Answer in Japanese. 文章展開 （各3点）

　・ _____

　・ _____

　・ _____

3. The word (3)crashed means ☐. 修辞 （6点）
　a. collided with something　　　b. decreased dramatically
　c. increased drastically　　　　d. pressed something

4. Translate the following into Japanese: (4)It is the use of these chemicals in Sichuan that has led to the loss of the insects that used to pollinate the apple trees. 知識・技能 （7点）

_____

_____

5. Who are the (5)people who would prefer to live without such "creepy crawlies"? Explain in English. 言いかえ表現 （7点）
They are people who _____.

6. Translate the following into Japanese: (6)if insects were to disappear completely, it would have almost unimaginable consequences for life on our planet. 知識・技能 （7点）

_____

_____

7. What is meant by (7)our small, struggling six-legged friends? Answer in one English word. 修辞 （7点）

_____

Lesson 18	語数(速読目標時間)	関連教科	関連SDGs	得 点
	571(5分40秒)	公民・家庭	12 RESPONSIBLE CONSUMPTION AND PRODUCTION ∞	
	制限時間			
	20分			/ 50

1 When shopping, most people probably focus on the price of the products. However, while low product prices are beneficial for consumers in the short term, they are not a wise choice in the long run if they have a negative impact on the environment. In recent years, an increasing number of consumers have been choosing products based on whether they are environmentally friendly or biodiversity-friendly. This consumption behavior is also known as "ethical consumption" and is being recommended worldwide. However, it is not so easy for consumers to choose environmentally friendly products.

2 Globally, many people now consider environmental issues to be very serious. This is why more and more consumers are likely to make "environmentally friendly" choices. However, (1)with this transition, there are also concerns that companies will label non-sustainable products sustainable in order to meet consumer demand. Consumers need to be properly informed about global issues in order to make the right choices. Otherwise, they may be worsening rather than helping to solve these problems.

3 Take the word "(2)organic" as an example. Many people may associate it with "environmentally friendly," but it should be noted that in some ways this is true and in other ways it is false. It is true that organic produce does not use chemical fertilizers; it prevents soil and river pollution and protects the ecosystem. On the other hand, organic produce requires more farmland than non-organic produce to yield the same amount. This leads to further deforestation and consequently to an increase in carbon dioxide emissions. It is also harmful to the ecosystem, as the reduction in forest area deprives the forest of habitats for the creatures that live there.

4 (3)Palm oil is an example of an agricultural product that, contrary to "organic," has a "bad for the environment" image among consumers. Palm oil is highly *versatile and is used in many food products, such as bread and crisps, and is said to be found in about half of all supermarket products. It is also used in *detergents and soaps. As the world's population grows, the demand for palm oil will *soar. The problem is that palm oil is produced in tropical regions; the expansion of oil palm plantations leads to deforestation. This has resulted in global criticism and even boycotts of palm oil. However, palm oil is characterized by its high production efficiency. Replacing it with other vegetable oils would require larger plantations and the alternative oils are not as versatile. There are ongoing efforts to produce palm oil sustainably, and it is

本文音声

considered more environmentally responsible to cooperate with these efforts than to
35 seek alternative oils.

5 To meet the needs of consumers who want to choose environmentally friendly products, it is essential for not only companies to be accountable, but also for government bodies to take action. One such initiative is (4)certification labels. These include labels showing that products have been grown on sustainable farms and labels
40 for seafood from sustainable fisheries. Such certification systems provide *transparency and help consumers make informed choices.

6 Consumers need to continue to educate themselves so that they can adopt the correct consumption behavior and not just be attracted by the phrase "environmentally friendly." To take a familiar example, eco-bags emit 50- 150 times more greenhouse
45 gases during production than plastic bags. To make eco-bags truly eco-friendly, it is not enough to just buy them and be happy with them: X

---

versatile：汎用性がある   detergent：洗剤   soar：急増する   transparency：透明性

次ページへ続く➡

1. Translate the following into Japanese: (1)with this transition, there are also concerns that companies will label non-sustainable products sustainable in order to meet consumer demand. Be sure to make "this transition" clear.　　🔖知識・技能 (9点)

_____

_____

2. When the word (2)organic is used in products, it necessarily means ⬚.　　🔖キーワード (7点)
   a. they are produced in environmentally friendly ways
   b. they are produced without chemical fertilizers
   c. they are qualified by the government
   d. they are still alive

3. Why do consumers have bad image of (3)palm oil? Explain in Japanese.　　🔖段落構成 (10点)

_____

_____

4. Which of the following best expresses the author's attitude toward (3)palm oil?　🔖段落構成 (7点)
   a. It is good to use palm oil as it is useful and other oils may be less environmentally friendly.
   b. It is sad that some people are still encouraging people to use it.
   c. Only palm oil should be used because other oils cost too much when produced.
   d. We should stop using it as soon as possible because producing it leads to deforestation.

5. According to the text, which of the following is an example of (4)certification labels?
   　　🔖応用 (7点)

a. 　　　　　b. 　　　　　c. 　　　　　d.

6. Write a suitable English sentence to fill in ⬚ X ⬚.　　🔖論理 (10点)

_____

_____

他の教科等に関連する語句特集

他の教科等で学習する内容を，英語を用いて課題解決することで，英語だけでなく，その内容に対する理解が深まります。ここでは，他の教科等で学習する内容を，学習指導要領などからピックアップしました。

国語　Japanese Language

☐ **Chinese character** [tʃàiníːz kǽrəktər] 名 「漢字」
▶common Kanji「常用漢字」。

☐ **classic** [klǽsɪk] 名 「古典」
▶classical Japanese literature とも表される。教科を表す際は classics（複数形）の形で表される。

☐ **colloquial** [kəlóʊkwiəl] 形 「口語の」
▶「話し言葉の」。

☐ **literary** [lítərèri] 形 「文語の」
▶「書き言葉の」。

☐ **context** [kántekst] 名 「文脈」

☐ **metaphor** [métəfɔ̀ːr] 名 「比喩」
▶Life is a river. 「人生は川のようだ。」のような，別のものに例えた表現。

☐ **euphemistic** [jùːfəmístɪk] 形 「婉曲的」
▶I am between jobs. 「失業中だ。」のような，遠まわしな表現。

☐ **rhetoric** [rétərɪk] 名 「修辞」
▶豊かな表現をするための文章表現の総称で，上記 metaphor や euphemistic expression, inversion「倒置法」などが含まれる。

地理歴史　Geography and History

☐ **disaster** [dɪzǽstər] 名 「災害」
▶台風や水害などの natural disaster や，人為的な原因によって起こる火事や事故を指す場合も使用される。an air disaster「航空機の大惨事」。

☐ **hazard map** [hǽzərd mǽp] 名 「ハザードマップ」
▶「災害予想図」。自然災害による被害の軽減や防災対策に使用する目的で，被災想定区域や避難場所・避難経路などの防災関係施設の位置などを表示した地図。

☐ **topography** [təpágrəfi] 名 「地形図」
▶等高線や色を使って高度や土地の形態を表す図。

☐ **modernization** [màdərnəzéɪʃ(ə)n] 名 「近代化」
▶modernize 動「…を近代化する」。

☐ **popularization** [pàpjələrəzéɪʃ(ə)n] 名 「大衆化」
▶popularize 動「…を大衆化する」。

☐ **material** [mətí(ə)riəl] 名 「資料」

公民　Civics

☐ **sovereignty** [sáv(ə)rənti] 名 「主権」
▶sovereignty of the people「国民主権」。

☐ **productive age** [prədʌ́ktɪv -] 名 「生産年齢」
▶生産活動に従事することのできる年齢。一般的に15歳〜64歳を指す。

☐ **voting** [vóʊtɪŋ] 名 「投票」
▶election「選挙」。presidential election「大統領選」。

☐ **contract** [kántrækt] 名 「契約」
▶上記の「投票」など，成人年齢引き下げにともない，18歳から親の同意なくできるようになったことのひとつに，（ローンや携帯電話などの）契約締結がある。

☐ **consumer** [kənsjúːmər] 名 「消費者」
▶consume 動「…を消費する」。

☐ **security** [sɪkjʊ́(ə)rəti] 名 「安全保障」
▶国家の安全保障について言うとき，特に national security と表記する場合もある。

☐ **EEZ** [íːíːzíː] 名 「排他的経済水域」
▶Exclusive Economic Zone の略。
▶領海（territorial sea）の外側，領海の基線から200海里（nautical miles）内で認められる主権的権利を持つ水域。

☐ **employment** [ɪmplɔ́ɪmənt] 名 「雇用」
▶employ 動「…を雇用する」，employer 名「雇用主」，employee 名「従業員」。

数学　Mathematics

☐ **data analysis** [- ənǽlɪsɪs] 名 「データの分析」
▶analysis「分析」。複数形は analyses [ənǽlɪsìːz]。

☐ **formula** [fɔ́ːrmjələ] 名 「公式」
▶the formula for calculating distance「距離を計算する公式」

☐ **equation** [ɪkwéɪʒ(ə)n] 名 「方程式」

☐ **shape** [ʃéɪp] 名 「図形」
▶「図形」全般を表す際は複数形で表される。

☐ **function** [fʌ́ŋkʃ(ə)n] 名 「関数」
▶「関数」全般を表す際は複数形で表される。

理科　Science

☐ **observation** [àbzərvéɪʃ(ə)n] 名 「観察」
▶observe 動「…を観察する」。知覚動詞で，ほかにも「…に気づく」「…を述べる」「…を遵守する」などの意味をもつ多義語である。

☐ **hypothesis** [haɪpάθəsɪs] 名 「仮説」
▶複数形は hypotheses [haɪpάθəsìːz]。

☐ **phenomenon** [fɪnάmənàn] 名 「現象」
▶複数形は phenomena [fɪnάmənə]。

☐ **particle** [pάːrtɪk(ə)l] 名 「粒子」

☐ **mass** [mǽs] 名 「質量」
▶物質の動きにくさ，慣性の大きさ。質量は地球上でも宇宙空間でも変わらない。単位は kg。

☐ **(aqueous) solution** [((éɪkwiəs) səlúːʃ(ə)n] 名 「水溶液」
▶saturated aqueous solution「飽和水溶液」。

☐ **ecosystem** [íːkoʊsìstəm] 名 「生態系」
▶太陽光のエネルギーを源とした，生物とそれらを取り巻く環境がお互いに関わり合う体系。

保健体育　Health and Physical Education

☐ **lifelong sport** [láɪflɔ̀ːŋ -] 名 「生涯スポーツ」
▶競うことよりも，生涯に渡って健康的な体を維持することを目的としたスポーツ。

☐ **first aid** [- éɪd] 名 「応急手当」
▶first-aid の形で使用されることもある。
▶形容詞としても使われる。first-aid kit「救急箱」。

☐ **cardiopulmonary resuscitation**
[kàrdiəpúlmənəri rɪsʌ̀sɪtéɪʃ(ə)n] 名 「心肺蘇生法」
▶cardiopulmonary 形「心肺の」，resuscitation 名「蘇生」。

☐ **AED** 名 「自動体外式除細動器」
▶Automated External Defibrillator の略。単に Defibrillator と呼ばれることもある。

☐ **lifestyle disease** [- dɪzíːz] 名 「生活習慣病」
▶病気全般を表す際は複数形で表される。食事や運動，休養，喫煙，飲酒などの生活習慣が深く関与し，それらが発症の要因となる疾患の総称。

家庭　Home Economics

☐ **food, clothing and shelter** 名 「衣食住」
▶necessities of life を「衣食住」と訳す場合もある。

☐ **welfare** [wélfèər] 名 「福祉」

☐ **consumption** [kənsʌ́mpʃ(ə)n] 名 「消費」
▶consumption tax「消費税」。

☐ **household** [háʊshòʊld] 名 「世帯」

情報　Information

☐ **information moral** [- mɔ́ːrəl] 名 「情報モラル」

☐ **information literacy** [- lít(ə)rəsi] 名 「情報リテラシー」
▶セキュリティや倫理的な問題を含む情報の処理能力を指すことが多い。

☐ **programming** [próʊgræmɪŋ] 名 「プログラミング」

☐ **simulate** [símjəlèɪt] 動 「…のシミュレーション[模擬実験]をする」

☐ **big data** [- déɪtə] 名 「ビッグデータ」
▶全体を把握することが困難な巨大なデータ群。